Japanese Text and English Translation
of
The Constitution of Japan

by

Kentaro Sato

2012

THE INTERNATIONAL UNLIMITED PRESS

JAPANESE TEXT AND ENGLISH TRANSLATION
OF
THE CONSTITUTION OF JAPAN

by Kentaro Sato

2nd Edition

First Printing: 2012

ISBN-10: 1481279394

ISBN-13 (EAN-13): 978-1481279390

Published by **The International Unlimited Press:**

a division of Aegis Shield Ltd. Co.   ©2012 Kentaro Sato   All Rights Reserved

Preface

The current Constitution of Japan was promulgated on November 3, 1946, and came into effect on May 3, 1947. As of December 17, 2012, it has not been amended.

The Constitution is founded on three fundamental principles: popular sovereignty, respect for fundamental human rights, and pacifism. Enacted after World War II, it played a pivotal role in Japan's democratization and the establishment of a peaceful society. It guarantees the rights and freedoms of the people and affirms that the nation's political structure is determined by its citizens. Additionally, it renounces war, prohibits the maintenance of military forces, and aims to uphold lasting peace.

Key features of the Constitution of Japan include:
- **Popular Sovereignty and the Emperor as the Symbol of the State:**
  The Constitution affirms that all political power resides with the people. The Emperor is defined as the symbol of the State and the unity of the people, with a strictly ceremonial role and no governing powers, reflecting Japan's democratic system.
- **Respect for Fundamental Human Rights:**
  Guarantees protection of basic human rights, including individual dignity and the rights to life, liberty, and the pursuit of happiness.
- **Pacifism:**
  Declares the renunciation of war, prohibits the maintenance of armed forces, and denies the right of belligerency, aiming to secure enduring peace.

The Constitution remains the foundation of Japan's democracy and pacifist ideals, playing a vital role in protecting the rights and freedoms of its people. Although the Preamble is not legally binding since it is not part of the Constitution's main body, it is regarded as an important expression of its guiding principles, summarizing the Constitution as a whole.

NOTE:
The Japanese text has been revised in accordance with the modern writing system—the modern kana orthography (*Gendai Kanazukai*, 現代仮名遣い)—and is supplemented with ruby characters (*furigana* 振り仮名) to facilitate reader comprehension.

Kentaro Sato

iii

目次　**Table of Contents**

日本国憲法　The Constitution of Japan

（にほんこくけんぽう）

ruby: 日本国憲法 → にほんこくけんぽう

前文　Preamble

日本国民は、正当に選挙された国会における代表者を通じて行動し、われらとわれらの子孫のために、諸国民との協和による成果と、わが国全土にわたって自由のもたらす恵沢を確保し、政府の行為によって再び戦争の惨禍が起ることのないようにすることを決意し、ここに主権が国民に存することを宣言し、この憲法を確定する。そもそも国政は、国民の厳粛な信託によるものであって、その権威は国民に由来し、その権力は国民の代表者がこれを行使し、その福利は国民がこれを享受する。これは人類普遍の原理であり、この憲法は、かかる原理に基くものである。われらは、これに反する一切の憲法、法令及び詔勅[1]を排除する。

We, the Japanese people, acting through our duly elected representatives in the National Diet, determined that we shall secure for ourselves and our posterity the fruits of peaceful cooperation with all nations and the blessings of liberty throughout this land, and resolved that never again shall we be visited with the horrors of war through the action of government, do proclaim that sovereign power resides with the people and do firmly establish this Constitution. Government is a sacred trust of the people, the authority for which is derived from the people, the powers of which are exercised by the representatives of the people, and the benefits of which are enjoyed by the people. This is a universal principle of

---

[1] 天皇が文書で行う行為。(Acts performed by the Emperor in writing.)

mankind upon which this Constitution is founded. We reject and revoke all constitutions, laws, ordinances, and rescripts in conflict herewith.

日本国民は、恒久の平和を念願し、人間相互の関係を支配する崇高な理想を深く自覚するのであって、平和を愛する諸国民の公正と信義に信頼して、われらの安全と生存を保持しようと決意した。われらは、平和を維持し、専制と隷従、圧迫と偏狭を地上から永遠に除去しようと努めている国際社会において、名誉ある地位を占めたいと思う。われらは、全世界の国民が、ひとしく恐怖と欠乏から免がれ、平和のうちに生存する権利を有することを確認する。

We, the Japanese people, desire peace for all time and are deeply conscious of the high ideals controlling human relationship, and we have determined to preserve our security and existence, trusting in the justice and faith of the peace-loving peoples of the world. We desire to occupy an honored place in an international society striving for the preservation of peace, and the banishment of tyranny and slavery, oppression and intolerance for all time from the earth. We recognize that all peoples of the world have the right to live in peace, free from fear and want.

われらは、いずれの国家も、自国のことのみに専念して他国を無視してはならないのであって、政治道徳の法則は、普遍的なものであ

り、この法則に従うことは、自国の主権を維持し、他国と対等関係に立とうとする各国の責務であると信ずる。

We believe that no nation is responsible to itself alone, but that laws of political morality are universal; and that obedience to such laws is incumbent upon all nations who would sustain their own sovereignty and justify their sovereign relationship with other nations.

日本国民は、国家の名誉にかけ、全力をあげてこの崇高な理想と目的を達成することを誓う。

We, the Japanese people, pledge our national honor to accomplish these high ideals and purposes with all our resources.

第一章　天皇 Chapter I. The Emperor

第一条　天皇は、日本国の象徴であり日本国民統合の象徴であって、この地位は、主権の存する日本国民の総意に基く。

Article 1. The Emperor shall be the symbol of the State and of the unity of the people, deriving his position from the will of the people with whom resides sovereign power.

第二条　皇位は、世襲のものであって、国会の議決した皇室典範の定めるところにより、これを継承する。

Article 2. The Imperial Throne shall be dynastic and succeeded to in accordance with the Imperial House Law passed by the Diet.

第三条　天皇の国事に関するすべての行為には、内閣の助言と承認を必要とし、内閣が、その責任を負う。

Article 3. The advice and approval of the Cabinet shall be required for all acts of the Emperor in matters of state, and the Cabinet shall be responsible therefor.

第四条　天皇は、この憲法の定める国事に関する行為のみを行い、国政に関する権能を有しない。

Article 4. The Emperor shall perform only such acts in matters of state as are provided for in this Constitution and he shall not have powers related to government.

天皇は、法律の定めるところにより、その国事に関する行為を委任することができる。

The Emperor may delegate the performance of his acts in matters of state as may be provided by law.

第五条　皇室典範の定めるところにより摂政を置くときは、摂政は、天皇の名でその国事に関する行為を行う。この場合には、前条第一項の規定を準用する。

Article 5. When, in accordance with the Imperial House Law, a Regency is established, the Regent shall perform his acts in matters of state in the Emperor's name. In this case, paragraph one of the preceding article will be applicable.

第六条　天皇は、国会の指名に基いて、内閣総理大臣を任命する。

Article 6. The Emperor shall appoint the Prime Minister as designated by the Diet.

天皇は、内閣の指名に基いて、最高裁判所の長たる裁判官を任命する。

The Emperor shall appoint the Chief Judge of the Supreme Court as designated by the Cabinet.

第七条　天皇は、内閣の助言と承認により、国民のために、左[2]の国事に関する行為を行う。

Article 7. The Emperor, with the advice and approval of the Cabinet, shall perform the following acts in matters of state on behalf of the people:

一　憲法改正、法律、政令及び条約を公布すること。

1. Promulgation of amendments of the constitution, laws, cabinet orders and treaties.

二　国会を召集すること。

2. Convocation of the Diet.

三　衆議院を解散すること。

3. Dissolution of the House of Representatives.

四　国会議員の総選挙の施行を公示すること。

4. Proclamation of general election of members of the Diet.

五　国務大臣及び法律の定めるその他の官吏の任免並びに全権委任状及び大使及び公使の信任状を認証すること。

---

[2] 原文が縦書きのため「左」は、以下の一から十までのことを指す。

5. Attestation of the appointment and dismissal of Ministers of State and other officials as provided for by law, and of full powers and credentials of Ambassadors and Ministers.

六　大赦、特赦、減刑、刑の執行の免除及び復権を認証すること。

6. Attestation of general and special amnesty, commutation of punishment, reprieve, and restoration of rights.

七　栄典を授与すること。

7. Awarding of honors.

八　批准書及び法律の定めるその他の外交文書を認証すること。

8. Attestation of instruments of ratification and other diplomatic documents as provided for by law.

九　外国の大使及び公使を接受すること。

9. Receiving foreign ambassadors and ministers.

十　儀式を行うこと。

10. Performance of ceremonial functions.

第八条　皇室に財産を譲り渡し、又は皇室が、財産を譲り受け、若しくは賜与することは、国会の議決に基かなければならない。

Article 8. No property can be given to, or received by, the Imperial House, nor can any gifts be made therefrom, without the authorization of the Diet.

第二章　戦争の放棄 Chapter II. Renunciation of War

第九条　日本国民は、正義と秩序を基調とする国際平和を誠実に希求し、国権の発動たる戦争と、武力による威嚇又は武力の行使は、国際紛争を解決する手段としては、永久にこれを放棄する。

Article 9. Aspiring sincerely to an international peace based on justice and order, the Japanese people forever renounce war as a sovereign right of the nation and the threat or use of force as means of settling international disputes.

前項の目的を達するため、陸海空軍その他の戦力は、これを保持しない。国の交戦権は、これを認めない。

In order to accomplish the aim of the preceding paragraph, land, sea, and air forces, as well as other war potential, will never be maintained. The right of belligerency of the state will not be recognized.

第三章　国民の権利及び義務 Chapter III. Rights and Duties of the People

第十条　日本国民たる要件は、法律でこれを定める。

Article 10. The conditions necessary for being a Japanese national shall be determined by law.

第十一条　国民は、すべての基本的人権の享有を妨げられない。この憲法が国民に保障する基本的人権は、侵すことのできない永久の権利として、現在及び将来の国民に与えられる。

Article 11. The people shall not be prevented from enjoying any of the fundamental human rights. These fundamental human rights guaranteed to the people by this Constitution shall be conferred upon the people of this and future generations as eternal and inviolate rights.

第十二条　この憲法が国民に保障する自由及び権利は、国民の不断の努力によつて、これを保持しなければならない。又、国民は、これを濫用してはならないのであつて、常に公共の福祉のためにこれを利用する責任を負う。

Article 12. The freedoms and rights guaranteed to the people by this Constitution shall be maintained by the constant endeavor of the people, who shall refrain from any abuse of these freedoms and rights and shall always be responsible for utilizing them for the public welfare.

第十三条　すべて国民は、個人として尊重される。生命、自由及び幸福追求に対する国民の権利については、公共の福祉に反しない限り、立法その他の国政の上で、最大の尊重を必要とする。

Article 13. All of the people shall be respected as individuals. Their right to life, liberty, and the pursuit of happiness shall, to the extent that it does not interfere with the public welfare, be the supreme consideration in legislation and in other governmental affairs.

第十四条 すべて国民は、法の下に平等であって、人種、信条、性別、社会的身分又は門地により、政治的、経済的又は社会的関係において、差別されない。

Article 14. All of the people are equal under the law and there shall be no discrimination in political, economic or social relations because of race, creed, sex, social status or family origin.

華族その他の貴族の制度は、これを認めない。

Peers and peerage shall not be recognized.

栄誉、勲章その他の栄典の授与は、いかなる特権も伴わない。栄典の授与は、現にこれを有し、又は将来これを受ける者の一代に限り、その効力を有する。

No privilege shall accompany any award of honor, decoration or any distinction, nor shall any such award be valid beyond the lifetime of the individual who now holds or hereafter may receive it.

第十五条 公務員を選定し、及びこれを罷免することは、国民固有の権利である。

Article 15. The people have the inalienable right to choose their public officials and to dismiss them.

すべて公務員は、全体の奉仕者であって、一部の奉仕者ではない。

All public officials are servants of the whole community and not of any group thereof.

公務員の選挙については、成年者による普通選挙を保障する。

Universal adult suffrage is guaranteed with regard to the election of public officials.

すべて選挙における投票の秘密は、これを侵してはならない。選挙人は、その選択に関し公的にも私的にも責任を問われない。

In all elections, secrecy of the ballot shall not be violated. A voter shall not be answerable, publicly or privately, for the choice he has made.

第十六条　何人も、損害の救済、公務員の罷免、法律、命令又は規則の制定、廃止又は改正その他の事項に関し、平穏に請願する権利を有し、何人も、かかる請願をしたためにいかなる差別待遇も受けない。

Article 16. Every person shall have the right of peaceful petition for the redress of damage, for the removal of public officials, for the enactment, repeal or amendment of laws, ordinances or regulations and for other matters; nor shall any person be in any way discriminated against for sponsoring such a petition.

第十七条　何人も、公務員の不法行為により、損害を受けたときは、法律の定めるところにより、国又は公共団体に、その賠償を求めることができる。

Article 17. Every person may sue for redress as provided by law from the State or a public entity, in case he has suffered damage through illegal act of any public official.

第十八条　何人も、いかなる奴隷的拘束も受けない。又、犯罪に因る処罰の場合を除いては、その意に反する苦役に服させられない。

Article 18. No person shall be held in bondage of any kind. Involuntary servitude, except as punishment for crime, is prohibited.

第十九条　思想及び良心の自由は、これを侵してはならない。

Article 19. Freedom of thought and conscience shall not be violated.

第二十条　信教の自由は、何人に対してもこれを保障する。いかなる宗教団体も、国から特権を受け、又は政治上の権力を行使してはならない。

Article 20. Freedom of religion is guaranteed to all. No religious organization shall receive any privileges from the State, nor exercise any political authority.

何人も、宗教上の行為、祝典、儀式又は行事に参加することを強制されない。

No person shall be compelled to take part in any religious act, celebration, rite or practice.

国及びその機関は、宗教教育その他いかなる宗教的活動もしてはならない。

The State and its organs shall refrain from religious education or any other religious activity.

第二十一条　集会、結社及び言論、出版その他一切の表現の自由は、これを保障する。

Article 21. Freedom of assembly and association as well as speech, press and all other forms of expression are guaranteed.

20

検閲は、これをしてはならない。通信の秘密は、これを侵してはならない。

No censorship shall be maintained, nor shall the secrecy of any means of communication be violated.

第二十二条　何人も、公共の福祉に反しない限り、居住、移転及び職業選択の自由を有する。

Article 22. Every person shall have freedom to choose and change his residence and to choose his occupation to the extent that it does not interfere with the public welfare.

何人も、外国に移住し、又は国籍を離脱する自由を侵されない。

Freedom of all persons to move to a foreign country and to divest themselves of their nationality shall be inviolate.

第二十三条　学問の自由は、これを保障する。

Article 23. Academic freedom is guaranteed.

第二十四条　婚姻は、両性の合意のみに基いて成立し、夫婦が同等の権利を有することを基本として、相互の協力により、維持されなければならない。

Article 24. Marriage shall be based only on the mutual consent of both sexes and it shall be maintained through mutual cooperation with the equal rights of husband and wife as a basis.

配偶者の選択、財産権、相続、住居の選定、離婚並びに婚姻及び家族に関するその他の事項に関しては、法律は、個人の尊厳と両性の本質的平等に立脚して、制定されなければならない。

With regard to choice of spouse, property rights, inheritance, choice of domicile, divorce and other matters pertaining to marriage and the family, laws shall be enacted from the standpoint of individual dignity and the essential equality of the sexes.

第二十五条　すべて国民は、健康で文化的な最低限度の生活を営む権利を有する。

Article 25. All people shall have the right to maintain the minimum standards of wholesome and cultured living.

国は、すべての生活部面について、社会福祉、社会保障及び公衆衛生の向上及び増進に努めなければならない。

In all spheres of life, the State shall use its endeavors for the promotion and extension of social welfare and security, and of public health.

第二十六条　すべて国民は、法律の定めるところにより、その能力に応じて、ひとしく教育を受ける権利を有する。

Article 26. All people shall have the right to receive an equal education correspondent to their ability, as provided by law.

すべて国民は、法律の定めるところにより、その保護する子女に普通教育を受けさせる義務を負う。義務教育は、これを無償とする。

All people shall be obligated to have all boys and girls under their protection receive ordinary education as provided for by law. Such compulsory education shall be free.

第二十七条　すべて国民は、勤労の権利を有し、義務を負う。

Article 27. All people shall have the right and the obligation to work.

賃金、就業時間、休息その他の勤労条件に関する基準は、法律でこれを定める。

Standards for wages, hours, rest and other working conditions shall be fixed by law.

児童は、これを酷使してはならない。

Children shall not be exploited.

<ruby>第二十八条<rt>だいにじゅうはちじょう</rt></ruby> <ruby>勤労者<rt>きんろうしゃ</rt></ruby>の<ruby>団結<rt>だんけつ</rt></ruby>する<ruby>権利及<rt>けんりおよ</rt></ruby>び<ruby>団体<rt>だんたい</rt></ruby><ruby>交渉<rt>こうしょう</rt></ruby>その<ruby>他<rt>た</rt></ruby>の<ruby>団体行動<rt>だんたいこうどう</rt></ruby>をする<ruby>権利<rt>けんり</rt></ruby>は、これを<ruby>保障<rt>ほしょう</rt></ruby>する。

Article 28. The right of workers to organize and to bargain and act collectively is guaranteed.

<ruby>第二十九条<rt>だいにじゅうきゅうじょう</rt></ruby> <ruby>財産権<rt>ざいさんけん</rt></ruby>は、これを<ruby>侵<rt>おか</rt></ruby>してはならない。

Article 29. The right to own or to hold property is inviolable.

<ruby>財産権<rt>ざいさんけん</rt></ruby>の<ruby>内容<rt>ないよう</rt></ruby>は、<ruby>公共<rt>こうきょう</rt></ruby>の<ruby>福祉<rt>ふくし</rt></ruby>に<ruby>適合<rt>てきごう</rt></ruby>するように、<ruby>法律<rt>ほうりつ</rt></ruby>でこれを<ruby>定<rt>さだ</rt></ruby>める。

Property rights shall be defined by law, in conformity with the public welfare.

<ruby>私有財産<rt>しゆうざいさん</rt></ruby>は、<ruby>正当<rt>せいとう</rt></ruby>な<ruby>補償<rt>ほしょう</rt></ruby>の<ruby>下<rt>もと</rt></ruby>に、これを<ruby>公共<rt>こうきょう</rt></ruby>のために<ruby>用<rt>もち</rt></ruby>いることができる。

Private property may be taken for public use upon just compensation therefor.

第
だい
三
さん
十
じゅう
条
じょう
　国民
こくみん
は、法律
ほうりつ
の定
さだ
めるところにより、納税
のうぜい
の義務
ぎ む
を負
お
う。

Article 30. The people shall be liable to taxation as provided by law.

第
だい
三
さん
十
じゅう
一
いち
条
じょう
　何人
なんぴと
も、法律
ほうりつ
の定
さだ
める手続
てつづき
によらなければ、その生命
せいめい
若
も
しくは自由
じ ゆう
を奪
うば
われ、又
また
はその他
た
の刑罰
けいばつ
を科
か
せられない。

Article 31. No person shall be deprived of life or liberty, nor shall any other criminal penalty be imposed, except according to procedure established by law.

第
だい
三
さん
十
じゅう
二
に
条
じょう
　何人
なんぴと
も、裁判所
さいばんしょ
において裁判
さいばん
を受
う
ける権利
けんり
を奪
うば
われない。

Article 32. No person shall be denied the right of access to the courts.

第
だい
三
さん
十
じゅう
三
さん
条
じょう
　何人
なんぴと
も、現行犯
げんこうはん
として逮捕
たいほ
される場合
ばあい
を除
のぞ
いては、権限
けんげん
を有
ゆう
する司法官憲
しほうかんけん
が発
はっ
し、且
か
つ理由
りゆう
となっている犯罪
はんざい
を明示
めいじ
する令状
れいじょう
によらなければ、逮捕
たいほ
されない。

Article 33. No person shall be apprehended except upon warrant issued by a competent judicial officer which specifies the offense with which the person is charged, unless he is apprehended, the offense being committed.

第三十四条　何人も、理由を直ちに告げられ、且つ、直ちに弁護人に依頼する権利を与えられなければ、抑留又は拘禁されない。又、何人も、正当な理由がなければ、拘禁されず、要求があれば、その理由は、直ちに本人及びその弁護人の出席する公開の法廷で示されなければならない。

Article 34. No person shall be arrested or detained without being at once informed of the charges against him or without the immediate privilege of counsel; nor shall he be detained without adequate cause; and upon demand of any person such cause must be immediately shown in open court in his presence and the presence of his counsel.

第三十五条　何人も、その住居、書類及び所持品について、侵入、捜索及び押収を受けることのない権利は、第三十三条の場合を除いては、正当な理由に基いて発せられ、且つ捜索する場所及び押収する物を明示する令状がなければ、侵されない。

Article 35. The right of all persons to be secure in their homes, papers and effects against entries, searches and seizures shall not be impaired except upon warrant issued for adequate cause and particularly describing the place to be searched and things to be seized, or except as provided by Article 33.

捜索又は押収は、権限を有する司法官憲が発する各別の令状により、これを行う。

Each search or seizure shall be made upon separate warrant issued by a competent judicial officer.

第三十六条　公務員による拷問及び残虐な刑罰は、絶対にこれを禁ずる。

Article 36. The infliction of torture by any public officer and cruel punishments are absolutely forbidden.

第三十七条　すべて刑事事件においては、被告人は、公平な裁判所の迅速な公開裁判を受ける権利を有する。

Article 37. In all criminal cases the accused shall enjoy the right to a speedy and public trial by an impartial tribunal.

刑事被告人は、すべての証人に対して審問する機会を充分に与えられ、又、公費で自己のために強制的手続により証人を求める権利を有する。

He shall be permitted full opportunity to examine all witnesses, and he shall have the right of compulsory process for obtaining witnesses on his behalf at public expense.

刑事被告人は、いかなる場合にも、資格を有する弁護人を依頼することができる。被告人が自らこれを依頼することができないときは、国でこれを附する。

At all times the accused shall have the assistance of competent counsel who shall, if the accused is unable to secure the same by his own efforts, be assigned to his use by the State.

29

第三十八条　何人も、自己に不利益な供述を強要されない。

Article 38. No person shall be compelled to testify against himself.

強制、拷問若しくは脅迫による自白又は不当に長く抑留若しくは拘禁された後の自白は、これを証拠とすることができない。

Confession made under compulsion, torture or threat, or after prolonged arrest or detention shall not be admitted in evidence.

何人も、自己に不利益な唯一の証拠が本人の自白である場合には、有罪とされ、又は刑罰を科せられない。

No person shall be convicted or punished in cases where the only proof against him is his own confession.

第三十九条　何人も、実行の時に適法であった行為又は既に無罪とされた行為については、刑事上の責任を問われない。又、同一の犯罪について、重ねて刑事上の責任を問われない。

Article 39. No person shall be held criminally liable for an act which was lawful at the time it was committed, or of which he has been acquitted, nor shall he be placed in double jeopardy.

第四十条　何人も、抑留又は拘禁された後、無罪の裁判を受けたときは、法律の定めるところにより、国にその補償を求めることができる。

Article 40. Any person, in case he is acquitted after he has been arrested or detained, may sue the State for redress as provided by law.

第四章　国会 Chapter IV. The Diet

第四十一条　国会は、国権の最高機関であって、国の唯一の立法機関である。

Article 41. The Diet shall be the highest organ of state power, and shall be the sole law-making organ of the State.

第四十二条　国会は、衆議院及び参議院の両議院でこれを構成する。

Article 42. The Diet shall consist of two Houses, namely the House of Representatives and the House of Councilors.

第四十三条　両議院は、全国民を代表する選挙された議員でこれを組織する。

Article 43. Both Houses shall consist of elected members, representative of all the people.

両議院の議員の定数は、法律でこれを定める。

The number of the members of each House shall be fixed by law.

第四十四条　両議院の議員及びその選挙人の資格は、法律でこれを定める。但し、人種、信条、性別、社会的身分、門地、教育、財産又は収入によって差別してはならない。

Article 44. The qualifications of members of both Houses and their electors shall be fixed by law. However, there shall be no discrimination because of race, creed, sex, social status, family origin, education, property or income.

第四十五条　衆議院議員の任期は、四年とする。但し、衆議院解散の場合には、その期間満了前に終了する。

Article 45. The term of office of members of the House of Representatives shall be four years. However, the term shall be terminated before the full term is up in case the House of Representatives is dissolved.

第四十六条　参議院議員の任期は、六年とし、三年ごとに議員の半数を改選する。

Article 46. The term of office of members of the House of Councilors shall be six years, and election for half the members shall take place every three years.

第四十七条　選挙区、投票の方法その他両議院の議員の選挙に関する事項は、法律でこれを定める。

Article 47. Electoral districts, method of voting and other matters pertaining to the method of election of members of both Houses shall be fixed by law.

第四十八条　何人も、同時に両議院の議員たることはできない。

Article 48. No person shall be permitted to be a member of both Houses simultaneously.

第四十九条　両議院の議員は、法律の定めるところにより、国庫から相当額の歳費を受ける。

Article 49. Members of both Houses shall receive appropriate annual payment from the national treasury in accordance with law.

第五十条　両議院の議員は、法律の定める場合を除いては、国会の会期中逮捕されず、会期前に逮捕された議員は、その議院の要求があれば、会期中これを釈放しなければならない。

Article 50. Except in cases provided by law, members of both Houses shall be exempt from apprehension while the Diet is in session, and any members apprehended before the opening of the session shall be freed during the term of the session upon demand of the House.

第五十一条　両議院の議員は、議院で行った演説、討論又は表決について、院外で責任を問われない。

Article 51. Members of both Houses shall not be held liable outside the House for speeches, debates or votes cast inside the House.

第五十二条　国会の常会は、毎年一回これを召集する。

Article 52. An ordinary session of the Diet shall be convoked once per year.

第五十三条　内閣は、国会の臨時会の召集を決定することができる。いずれかの議院の総議員の四分の一以上の要求があれば、内閣は、その召集を決定しなければならない。

Article 53. The Cabinet may determine to convoke extraordinary sessions of the Diet. When a quarter or more of the total members of either House makes the demand, the Cabinet must determine on such convocation.

第五十四条　衆議院が解散されたときは、解散の日から四十日以内に、衆議院議員の総選挙を行い、その選挙の日から三十日以内に、国会を召集しなければならない。

Article 54. When the House of Representatives is dissolved, there must be a general election of members of the House of Representatives within forty (40) days from the date of dissolution, and the Diet must be convoked within thirty (30) days from the date of the election.

衆議院が解散されたときは、参議院は、同時に閉会となる。但し、内閣は、国に緊急の必要があるときは、参議院の緊急集会を求めることができる。

When the House of Representatives is dissolved, the House of Councilors is closed at the same time. However, the Cabinet may in time of national emergency convoke the House of Councilors in emergency session.

前項但書の緊急集会において採られた措置は、臨時のものであって、次の国会開会の後十日以内に、衆議院の同意がない場合には、その効力を失う。

Measures taken at such session as mentioned in the proviso of the preceding paragraph shall be provisional and shall become null and void unless agreed to by the House of Representatives within a period of ten (10) days after the opening of the next session of the Diet.

第五十五条　両議院は、各々その議員の資格に関する争訟を裁判する。但し、議員の議席を失わせるには、出席議員の三分の二以上の多数による議決を必要とする。

Article 55. Each House shall judge disputes related to qualifications of its members. However, in order to deny a seat to any member, it is necessary to pass a resolution by a majority of two-thirds or more of the members present.

第五十六条　両議院は、各々その総議員の三分の一以上の出席がなければ、議事を開き議決することができない。

Article 56. Business cannot be transacted in either House unless one-third or more of total membership is present.

両議院の議事は、この憲法に特別の定のある場合を除いては、出席議員の過半数でこれを決し、可否同数のときは、議長の決するところによる。

All matters shall be decided, in each House, by a majority of those present, except as elsewhere provided in the Constitution, and in case of a tie, the presiding officer shall decide the issue.

第五十七条　両議院の会議は、公開とする。但し、出席議員の三分の二以上の多数で議決したときは、秘密会を開くことができる。

Article 57. Deliberation in each House shall be public. However, a secret meeting may be held where a majority of two-thirds or more of those members present passes a resolution therefor.

両議院は、各々その会議の記録を保存し、秘密会の記録の中で特に秘密を要すると認められるもの以外は、これを公表し、且つ一般に頒布しなければならない。

Each House shall keep a record of proceedings. This record shall be published and given general circulation, excepting such parts of proceedings of secret session as may be deemed to require secrecy.

出席議員の五分の一以上の要求があれば、各議員の表決は、これを会議録に記載しなければならない。

Upon demand of one-fifth or more of the members present, votes of the members on any matter shall be recorded in the minutes.

第五十八条　両議院は、各々その議長その他の役員を選任する。

Article 58. Each House shall select its own president and other officials.

両議院は、各々その会議その他の手続及び内部の規律に関する規則を定め、又、院内の秩序をみだした議員を懲罰することができる。但し、議員を除名するには、出席議員の三分の二以上の多数による議決を必要とする。

Each House shall establish its rules pertaining to meetings, proceedings and internal discipline, and may punish members for disorderly conduct. However, in order to expel a member, a majority of two-thirds or more of those members present must pass a resolution thereon.

第五十九条　法律案は、この憲法に特別の定のある場合を除いては、両議院で可決したとき法律となる。

Article 59. A bill becomes a law on passage by both Houses, except as otherwise provided by the Constitution.

衆議院で可決し、参議院でこれと異なった議決をした法律案は、衆議院で出席議員の三分の二以上の多数で再び可決したときは、法律となる。

A bill which is passed by the House of Representatives, and upon which the House of Councilors makes a decision different from that of the House of Representatives, becomes a law when passed a second time by the House of Representatives by a majority of two-thirds or more of the members present.

前項の規定は、法律の定めるところにより、衆議院が、両議院の協議会を開くことを求めることを妨げない。

The provision of the preceding paragraph does not preclude the House of Representatives from calling for the meeting of a joint committee of both Houses, provided for by law.

参議院が、衆議院の可決した法律案を受け取った後、国会休会中の期間を除いて六十日以内に、議決しないときは、衆議院は、参議院がその法律案を否決したものとみなすことができる。

Failure by the House of Councilors to take final action within sixty (60) days after receipt of a bill passed by the House of Representatives, time in recess excepted, may be determined by the House of Representatives to constitute a rejection of the said bill by the House of Councilors.

第六十条 予算は、さきに衆議院に提出しなければならない。

Article 60. The budget must first be submitted to the House of Representatives.

予算について、参議院で衆議院と異なった議決をした場合に、法律の定めるところにより、両議院の協議会を開いても意見が一致しないとき、又は参議院が、衆議院の可決した予算を受け取った後、国会休会中の期間を除いて三十日以内に、議決しないときは、衆議院の議決を国会の議決とする。

Upon consideration of the budget, when the House of Councilors makes a decision different from that of the House of Representatives, and when no agreement can be reached even through a joint committee of both Houses, provided for by law, or in the case of failure by the House of Councilors to take final action within thirty (30) days, the period of recess excluded, after the receipt of the budget passed by the House of Representatives, the decision of the House of Representatives shall be the decision of the Diet.

第六十一条　条約の締結に必要な国会の承認については、前条第二項の規定を準用する。

Article 61. The second paragraph of the preceding article applies also to the Diet approval required for the conclusion of treaties.

第六十二条　両議院は、各々国政に関する調査を行い、これに関して、証人の出頭及び証言並びに記録の提出を要求することができる。

Article 62. Each House may conduct investigations in relation to government, and may demand the presence and testimony of witnesses, and the production of records.

第六十三条　内閣総理大臣その他の国務大臣は、両議院の一つに議席を有すると有しないとにかかわらず、何時でも議案について発言するため議院に出席することができる。又、答弁又は説明のため出席を求められたときは、出席しなければならない。

Article 63. The Prime Minister and other Ministers of State may, at any time, appear in either House for the purpose of speaking on bills, regardless of whether they are members of the House or not. They must appear when their presence is required in order to give answers or explanations.

第六十四条　国会は、罷免の訴追を受けた裁判官を裁判するため、両議院の議員で組織する弾劾裁判所を設ける。

Article 64. The Diet shall set up an impeachment court from among the members of both Houses for the purpose of trying those judges against whom removal proceedings have been instituted.

弾劾に関する事項は、法律でこれを定める。

Matters relating to impeachment shall be provided by law

第五章　内閣 Chapter V. The Cabinet

第六十五条　行政権は、内閣に属する。

Article 65. Executive power shall be vested in the Cabinet.

第六十六条　内閣は、法律の定めるところにより、その首長たる内閣総理大臣及びその他の国務大臣でこれを組織する。

Article 66. The Cabinet shall consist of the Prime Minister, who shall be its head, and other Ministers of State, as provided for by law.

内閣総理大臣その他の国務大臣は、文民でなければならない。

The Prime Minister and other Ministers of State must be civilians.

内閣は、行政権の行使について、国会に対し連帯して責任を負う。

The Cabinet, in the exercise of executive power, shall be collectively responsible to the Diet.

第六十七条　内閣総理大臣は、国会議員の中から国会の議決で、これを指名する。この指名は、他のすべての案件に先だって、これを行う。

Article 67. The Prime Minister shall be designated from among the members of the Diet by a resolution of the Diet. This designation shall precede all other business.

衆議院と参議院とが異なった指名の議決をした場合に、法律の定めるところにより、両議院の協議会を開いても意見が一致しないとき、又は衆議院が指名の議決をした後、国会休会中の期間を除いて十日以内に、参議院が、指名の議決をしないときは、衆議院の議決を国会の議決とする。

If the House of Representatives and the House of Councilors disagree and if no agreement can be reached even through a joint committee of both Houses, provided for by law, or the House of Councilors fails to make designation within ten (10) days, exclusive of the period of recess, after the House of Representatives has made designation, the decision of the House of Representatives shall be the decision of the Diet.

第六十八条　内閣総理大臣は、国務大臣を任命する。但し、その過半数は、国会議員の中から選ばれなければならない。

Article 68. The Prime Minister shall appoint the Ministers of State. However, a majority of their number must be chosen from among the members of the Diet.

内閣総理大臣は、任意に国務大臣を罷免することができる。

The Prime Minister may remove the Ministers of State as he chooses.

第六十九条　内閣は、衆議院で不信任の決議案を可決し、又は信任の決議案を否決したときは、十日以内に衆議院が解散されない限り、総辞職をしなければならない。

Article 69. If the House of Representatives passes a non-confidence resolution, or rejects a confidence resolution, the Cabinet shall resign en masse, unless the House of Representatives is dissolved within ten (10) days.

第七十条　内閣総理大臣が欠けたとき、又は衆議院議員総選挙の後に初めて国会の召集があったときは、内閣は、総辞職をしなければならない。

Article 70. When there is a vacancy in the post of Prime Minister, or upon the first convocation of the Diet after a general election of members of the House of Representatives, the Cabinet shall resign en masse.

第七十一条　前二条[3]の場合には、内閣は、あらたに内閣総理大臣が任命されるまで引き続きその職務を行う。

Article 71. In the cases mentioned in the two preceding articles, the Cabinet shall continue its functions until the time when a new Prime Minister is appointed.

---

[3] 第六十九条、及び七十条 (Article 69 and Article 70)

第七十二条　内閣総理大臣は、内閣を代表して議案を国会に提出し、一般国務及び外交関係について国会に報告し、並びに行政各部を指揮監督する。

Article 72. The Prime Minister, representing the Cabinet, submits bills, reports on general national affairs and foreign relations to the Diet and exercises control and supervision over various administrative branches.

第七十三条　内閣は、他の一般行政事務の外、左[4]の事務を行う。

Article 73. The Cabinet, in addition to other general administrative functions, shall perform the following functions:

一　法律を誠実に執行し、国務を総理すること。

1. Administer the law faithfully; conduct affairs of state.

二　外交関係を処理すること。

2. Manage foreign affairs.

三　条約を締結すること。但し、事前に、時宜によつては事後に、国会の承認を経ることを必要とする。

---

[4]原文が縦書きのため「左」は、以下の一から七までのことを指す。

3. Conclude treaties. However, it shall obtain prior or, depending on circumstances, subsequent approval of the Diet.

四　法律の定める基準に従い、官吏に関する事務を掌理すること。

4. Administer the civil service, in accordance with standards established by law.

五　予算を作成して国会に提出すること。

5. Prepare the budget, and present it to the Diet.

六　この憲法及び法律の規定を実施するために、政令を制定すること。但し、政令には、特にその法律の委任がある場合を除いては、罰則を設けることができない。

6. Enact cabinet orders in order to execute the provisions of this Constitution and of the law. However, it cannot include penal provisions in such cabinet orders unless authorized by such law.

七　大赦、特赦、減刑、刑の執行の免除及び復権を決定すること。

7. Decide on general amnesty, special amnesty, commutation of punishment, reprieve, and restoration of rights.

第七十四条　法律及び政令には、すべて主任の国務大臣が署名し、内閣総理大臣が連署することを必要とする。

Article 74. All laws and cabinet orders shall be signed by the competent Minister of State and countersigned by the Prime Minister.

第七十五条　国務大臣は、その在任中、内閣総理大臣の同意がなければ、訴追されない。但し、これがため、訴追の権利は、害されない。

Article 75. The Ministers of State, during their tenure of office, shall not be subject to legal action without the consent of the Prime Minister. However, the right to take that action is not impaired hereby.

第六章　司法 Chapter VI. Judiciary

第七十六条　すべて司法権は、最高裁判所及び法律の定めるところにより設置する下級裁判所に属する。

Article 76. The whole judicial power is vested in a Supreme Court and in such inferior courts as are established by law.

特別裁判所は、これを設置することができない。行政機関は、終審として裁判を行うことができない。

No extraordinary tribunal shall be established, nor shall any organ or agency of the Executive be given final judicial power.

すべて裁判官は、その良心に従い独立してその職権を行い、この憲法及び法律にのみ拘束される。

All judges shall be independent in the exercise of their conscience and shall be bound only by this Constitution and the laws.

第七十七条　最高裁判所は、訴訟に関する手続、弁護士、裁判所の内部規律及び司法事務処理に関する事項について、規則を定める権限を有する。

Article 77. The Supreme Court is vested with the rule-making power under which it determines the rules of procedure and of practice, and of matters relating to attorneys, the internal discipline of the courts and the administration of judicial affairs.

検察官は、最高裁判所の定める規則に従わなければならない。

Public procurators shall be subject to the rule-making power of the Supreme Court.

最高裁判所は、下級裁判所に関する規則を定める権限を、下級裁判所に委任することができる。

The Supreme Court may delegate the power to make rules for inferior courts to such courts.

第七十八条　裁判官は、裁判により、心身の故障のために職務を執ることができないと決定された場合を除いては、公の弾劾によらなければ罷免されない。裁判官の懲戒処分は、行政機関がこれを行うことはできない。

Article 78. Judges shall not be removed except by public impeachment unless judicially declared mentally or physically incompetent to perform official duties. No disciplinary action against judges shall be administered by any executive organ or agency.

第七十九条　最高裁判所は、その長たる裁判官及び法律の定める員数のその他の裁判官でこれを構成し、その長たる裁判官以外の裁判官は、内閣でこれを任命する。

Article 79. The Supreme Court shall consist of a Chief Judge and such number of judges as may be determined by law; all such judges excepting the Chief Judge shall be appointed by the Cabinet.

最高裁判所の裁判官の任命は、その任命後初めて行われる衆議院議員総選挙の際国民の審査に付し、その後十年を経過した後初めて行われる衆議院議員総選挙の際更に審査に付し、その後も同様とする。

The appointment of the judges of the Supreme Court shall be reviewed by the people at the first general election of members of the House of Representatives following their appointment, and shall be reviewed again at the first general election of members of the House of Representatives after a lapse of ten (10) years, and in the same manner thereafter.

前項の場合において、投票者の多数が裁判官の罷免を可とするときは、その裁判官は、罷免される。

In cases mentioned in the foregoing paragraph, when the majority of the voters favors the dismissal of a judge, he shall be dismissed.

審査に関する事項は、法律でこれを定める。

Matters pertaining to review shall be prescribed by law.

最高裁判所の裁判官は、法律の定める年齢に達した時に退官する。

The judges of the Supreme Court shall be retired upon the attainment of the age as fixed by law.

最高裁判所の裁判官は、すべて定期に相当額の報酬を受ける。この報酬は、在任中、これを減額することができない。

All such judges shall receive, at regular stated intervals, adequate compensation which shall not be decreased during their terms of office.

第八十条　下級裁判所の裁判官は、最高裁判所の指名した者の名簿によって、内閣でこれを任命する。その裁判官は、任期を十年とし、再任されることができる。但し、法律の定める年齢に達した時には退官する。

Article 80. The judges of the inferior courts shall be appointed by the Cabinet from a list of persons nominated by the Supreme Court. All such judges shall hold office for a term of ten (10) years with privilege of reappointment, provided that they shall be retired upon the attainment of the age as fixed by law.

下級裁判所の裁判官は、すべて定期に相当額の報酬を受ける。この報酬は、在任中、これを減額することができない。

The judges of the inferior courts shall receive, at regular stated intervals, adequate compensation which shall not be decreased during their terms of office.

第八十一条　最高裁判所は、一切の法律、命令、規則又は処分が憲法に適合するかしないかを決定する権限を有する終審裁判所である。

Article 81. The Supreme Court is the court of last resort with power to determine the constitutionality of any law, order, regulation or official act.

第八十二条　裁判の対審及び判決は、公開法廷でこれを行う。

Article 82. Trials shall be conducted and judgment declared publicly.

裁判所が、裁判官の全員一致で、公の秩序又は善良の風俗を害する虞があると決した場合には、対審は、公開しないでこれを行うことができる。但し、政治犯罪、出版に関する犯罪又はこの憲法第三章で保障する国民の権利が問題となっている事件の対審は、常にこれを公開しなければならない。

Where a court unanimously determines publicity to be dangerous to public order or morals, a trial may be conducted privately, but trials of political offenses, offenses involving the press or cases wherein the rights of people as guaranteed in Chapter III of this Constitution are in question shall always be conducted publicly.

第七章　財政 Chapter VII. Finance

第八十三条　国の財政を処理する権限は、国会の議決に基いて、これを行使しなければならない。

Article 83. The power to administer national finances shall be exercised as the Diet shall determine.

第八十四条　あらたに租税を課し、又は現行の租税を変更するには、法律又は法律の定める条件によることを必要とする。

Article 84. No new taxes shall be imposed or existing ones modified except by law or under such conditions as law may prescribe.

第八十五条　国費を支出し、又は国が債務を負担するには、国会の議決に基くことを必要とする。

Article 85. No money shall be expended, nor shall the State obligate itself, except as authorized by the Diet.

第八十六条　内閣は、毎会計年度の予算を作成し、国会に提出して、その審議を受け議決を経なければならない。

Article 86. The Cabinet shall prepare and submit to the Diet for its consideration and decision a budget for each fiscal year.

第八十七条　予見し難い予算の不足に充てるため、国会の議決に基いて予備費を設け、内閣の責任でこれを支出することができる。

Article 87. In order to provide for unforeseen deficiencies in the budget, a reserve fund may be authorized by the Diet to be expended upon the responsibility of the Cabinet.

すべて予備費の支出については、内閣は、事後に国会の承諾を得なければならない。

The Cabinet must get subsequent approval of the Diet for all payments from the reserve fund.

第八十八条　すべて皇室財産は、国に属する。すべて皇室の費用は、予算に計上して国会の議決を経なければならない。

Article 88. All property of the Imperial Household shall belong to the State. All expenses of the Imperial Household shall be appropriated by the Diet in the budget.

第八十九条　公金その他の公の財産は、宗教上の組織若しくは団体の使用、便益若しくは維持のため、又は公の支配に属しない慈善、教育若しくは博愛の事業に対し、これを支出し、又はその利用に供してはならない。

Article 89. No public money or other property shall be expended or appropriated for the use, benefit or maintenance of any religious institution or association, or for any charitable, educational or benevolent enterprises not under the control of public authority.

第九十条　国の収入支出の決算は、すべて毎年会計検査院がこれを検査し、内閣は、次の年度に、その検査報告とともに、これを国会に提出しなければならない。

Article 90. Final accounts of the expenditures and revenues of the State shall be audited annually by a Board of Audit and submitted by the Cabinet to the Diet, together with the statement of audit, during the fiscal year immediately following the period covered.

会計検査院の組織及び権限は、法律でこれを定める。

The organization and competency of the Board of Audit shall be determined by law.

第九十一条　内閣は、国会及び国民に対し、定期に、少なくとも毎年一回、国の財政状況について報告しなければならない。

Article 91. At regular intervals and at least annually the Cabinet shall report to the Diet and the people on the state of national finances.

第八章　地方自治 Chapter VIII. Local Self-Government

第九十二条　地方公共団体の組織及び運営に関する事項は、地方自治の本旨に基いて、法律でこれを定める。

Article 92. Regulations concerning organization and operations of local public entities shall be fixed by law in accordance with the principle of local autonomy.

第九十三条　地方公共団体には、法律の定めるところにより、その議事機関として議会を設置する。

Article 93. The local public entities shall establish assemblies as their deliberative organs, in accordance with law.

地方公共団体の長、その議会の議員及び法律の定めるその他の吏員は、その地方公共団体の住民が、直接これを選挙する。

The chief executive officers of all local public entities, the members of their assemblies, and such other local officials as may be determined by law shall be elected by direct popular vote within their several communities.

第九十四条　地方公共団体は、その財産を管理し、事務を処理し、及び行政を執行する権能を有し、法律の範囲内で条例を制定することができる。

Article 94. Local public entities shall have the right to manage their property, affairs and administration and to enact their own regulations within law.

第九十五条　一つの地方公共団体のみに適用される特別法は、法律の定めるところにより、その地方公共団体の住民の投票においてその過半数の同意を得なければ、国会は、これを制定することができない。

Article 95. A special law, applicable only to one local public entity, cannot be enacted by the Diet without the consent of the majority of the voters of the local public entity concerned, obtained in accordance with law.

だいきゅうしょう　かいせい
第九章　改正 Chapter IX. Amendements

だいきゅうじゅうろくじょう　　　　　　　けんぽう　かいせい　　　　　かくぎいん　そうぎいん　さんぶん　にいじょう
第九十六条　この憲法の改正は、各議院の総議員の三分の二以上
さんせい　　こっかい　　　　　　　　　はつぎ　　　こくみん　ていあん　　　　　しょうにん　へ
の賛成で、国会が、これを発議し、国民に提案してその承認を経な
しょうにん　　　　とくべつ　こくみんとうひょうまた　こっかい　さだ
ければならない。この承認には、特別の国民投票又は国会の定め
せんきょ　さいおこな　　とうひょう　　　　　　　かはんすう　さんせい　ひつよう
る選挙の際行われる投票において、その過半数の賛成を必要とす
る。

Article 96. Amendments to this Constitution shall be initiated by the Diet, through a concurring vote of two-thirds or more of all the members of each House and shall thereupon be submitted to the people for ratification, which shall require the affirmative vote of a majority of all votes cast thereon, at a special referendum or at such election as the Diet shall specify.

けんぽうかいせい　　　　ぜんこう　しょうにん　へ　　　　　　てんのう　　こくみん
憲法改正について前項の承認を経たときは、天皇は、国民
な　　　　　けんぽう　いったい　な　　　　　　　　ただ
の名で、この憲法と一体を成すものとして、直ちにこれを
こうふ
公布する。

Amendments when so ratified shall immediately be promulgated by the Emperor in the name of the people, as an integral part of this Constitution.

第十章 最高法規 Chapter X. Supreme Law

第九十七条　この憲法が日本国民に保障する基本的人権は、人類の多年にわたる自由獲得の努力の成果であって、これらの権利は、過去幾多の試練5に堪え、現在及び将来の国民に対し、侵すことのできない永久の権利として信託されたものである。

Article 97. The fundamental human rights by this Constitution guaranteed to the people of Japan are fruits of the age-old struggle of man to be free; they have survived the many exacting tests for durability and are conferred upon this and future generations in trust, to be held for all time inviolate.

第九十八条　この憲法は、国の最高法規であって、その条規に反する法律、命令、詔勅及び国務に関するその他の行為の全部又は一部は、その効力を有しない。

Article 98. This Constitution shall be the supreme law of the nation and no law, ordinance, imperial rescript or other act of government, or part thereof, contrary to the provisions hereof, shall have legal force or validity.

---

5 試錬（原文）

日本国が締結した条約及び確立された国際法規は、これを誠実に遵守することを必要とする。

The treaties concluded by Japan and established laws of nations shall be faithfully observed.

第九十九条　天皇又は摂政及び国務大臣、国会議員、裁判官その他の公務員は、この憲法を尊重し擁護する義務を負う。

Article 99. The Emperor or the Regent as well as Ministers of State, members of the Diet, judges, and all other public officials have the obligation to respect and uphold this Constitution.

第十一章　補則 Chapter XI. Supplementary Provisions

第百条　この憲法は、公布の日から起算して六ヶ月⁶を経過した日から、これを施行する。

Article 100. This Constitution shall be enforced as from the day when the period of six months will have elapsed counting from the day of its promulgation.

この憲法を施行するために必要な法律の制定、参議院議員の選挙及び国会召集の手続並びにこの憲法を施行するために必要な準備手続は、前項の期日よりも前に、これを行うことができる。

The enactment of laws necessary for the enforcement of this Constitution, the election of members of the House of Councilors and the procedure for the convocation of the Diet and other preparatory procedures necessary for the enforcement of this Constitution may be executed before the day prescribed in the preceding paragraph.

---

⁶ 六箇月（原文）

第百一条　この憲法施行の際、参議院がまだ成立していないときは、その成立するまでの間、衆議院は、国会としての権限を行う。

Article 101. If the House of Councilors is not constituted before the effective date of this Constitution, the House of Representatives shall function as the Diet until such time as the House of Councilors shall be constituted.

第百二条　この憲法による第一期の参議院議員のうち、その半数の者の任期は、これを三年とする。その議員は、法律の定めるところにより、これを定める。

Article 102. The term of office for half the members of the House of Councilors serving in the first term under this Constitution shall be three years. Members falling under this category shall be determined in accordance with law.

第百三条 この憲法施行の際現に在職する国務大臣、衆議院議員及び裁判官並びにその他の公務員で、その地位に相応する地位がこの憲法で認められている者は、法律で特別の定をした場合を除いては、この憲法施行のため、当然にはその地位を失うことはない。但し、この憲法によつて、後任者が選挙又は任命されたときは、当然その地位を失う。

Article 103. The Ministers of State, members of the House of Representatives, and judges in office on the effective date of this Constitution, and all other public officials, who occupy positions corresponding to such positions as are recognized by this Constitution shall not forfeit their positions automatically on account of the enforcement of this Constitution unless otherwise specified by law. When, however, successors are elected or appointed under the provisions of this Constitution they shall forfeit their positions as a matter of course.

以上　End

Note:

Note:

www.ingramcontent.com/pod-product-compliance
Lightning Source LLC
Chambersburg PA
CBHW022130170526
45157CB00004B/1817

* 9 7 8 1 4 8 1 2 7 9 3 9 0 *